A Crabtree Branches Book

CATCH the Wave

LONGBOARD SURFING

Kerri Mazzarella

Crabtree Publishing
crabtreebooks.com

School-to-Home Support for Caregivers and Teachers

This high-interest book is designed to motivate striving students with engaging topics while building fluency, vocabulary, and an interest in reading. Here are a few questions and activities to help the reader build upon his or her comprehension skills.

Before Reading:

- *What do I think this book is about?*
- *What do I know about this topic?*
- *What do I want to learn about this topic?*
- *Why am I reading this book?*

During Reading:

- *I wonder why...*
- *I'm curious to know...*
- *How is this like something I already know?*
- *What have I learned so far?*

After Reading:

- *What was the author trying to teach me?*
- *What are some details?*
- *How did the photographs and captions help me understand more?*
- *Read the book again and look for the vocabulary words.*
- *What questions do I still have?*

Extension Activities:

- *What was your favorite part of the book? Write a paragraph on it.*
- *Draw a picture of your favorite thing you learned from the book.*

Table of Contents

WHAT IS LONGBOARD SURFING?

Longboard **surfing** is a watersport where a person uses a very long board to catch and ride waves in the ocean. A person who surfs is called a surfer.

Fact

Longboards are usually 8 to 10 feet (2.4 to 3 m) long.

Longboarding is a slow and relaxed style of surfing. It is very popular all over the world.

Longboard surfers enjoy riding small to medium waves, where they can glide along the water and show off their style and creativity.

Fact

Hang ten is a popular surfing trick in which the surfer walks to the front tip, or nose, of the surfboard and hangs all ten toes over the edge.

Longboarding is the oldest type of board surfing. It was started in **ancient** Polynesia and was later brought to Hawaii.

Fact

In 1907, longboarding was brought to Redondo Beach, California by a Hawaiian named George Freeth.

WHO CAN LONGBOARD SURF?

Longboarding is a fun activity for everyone! Both young and old people can learn to longboard.

Fact

You should be a strong swimmer before trying any type of surfing.

Fact

Spending time in the Sun safely provides your body with vitamin D.

Longboarding can provide many benefits to your overall health and wellbeing. It is a fun way to relieve stress, get exercise, and make new friends.

Fact

Learning different tricks and skills takes time and practice. Barrel or tube riding, shown above, is a challenging skill to learn.

Although anyone can longboard, some surfers take it more seriously than others. Longboarding can be a fun activity or a competitive sport.

CHOOSING YOUR EQUIPMENT

There are two main types of longboards, which allow for different longboard surfing styles.

Classic longboards, also known as logs or noseriders, are good for cruising smaller waves. They are wider for more **buoyancy** and allow the rider to walk on the board and hang ten!

High-performance longboards are used for tricks and quick turns. They are narrower to cut through larger waves. A high-performance longboard has more fins than a classic longboard.

One of the most important pieces of equipment for your longboard is a **leash**. You will also need surf wax and a traction pad to keep you from slipping off your board.

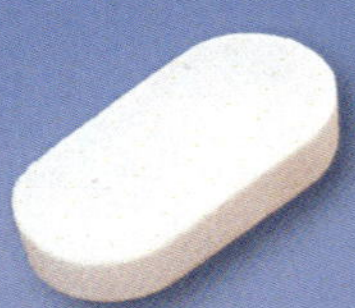

surf wax $5

leash $30–50

traction pad $30–80

Some surfers wear a **rash guard** to protect their skin from the board and the Sun. If the water is very cold, surfers may wear a **wetsuit**, booties, and gloves.

rash guard $20–80

wetsuit $70–200

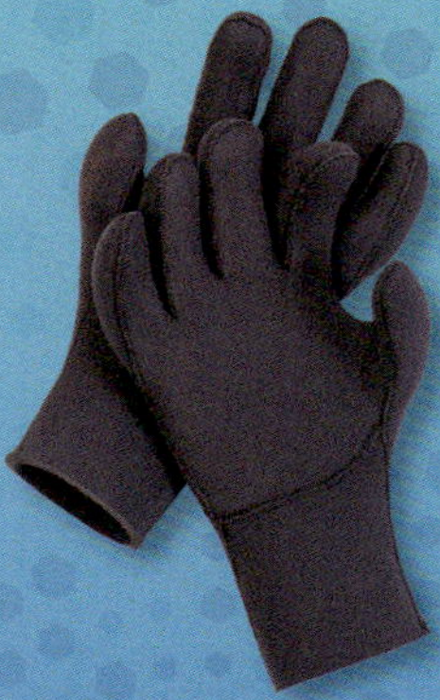

gloves $25–100

booties $50–100

WHERE TO LONGBOARD SURF

Longboarding can be done at almost any beach around the world. It is best for beginners to start in smaller waves.

Fact

Florida, California, and Hawaii all have great beaches for experienced and beginner longboarders in the U.S.

Fact

On beaches in California, the Black Ball flag is flown to tell surfers with surfboards that they cannot enter the water. This keeps swimmers safe from being hit by a surfboard.

Beginner longboarders should stay away from rocky beaches or **reefs**. These can cause harm to you and your board.

Beaches that have slow, rolling waves are best for beginners. It is best to avoid waves that break right on the beach. A break happens when the crest, or highest point, of a wave falls over onto itself.

HOW TO LONGBOARD SURF

Learning how to surf on a longboard is fun. Surfing requires core strength and good **balance**.

Fact

You can take longboarding lessons from a local instructor. It may cost around $50–150 per hour.

You will first need to learn how to "pop up." This is how a surfer moves from their stomach to their feet on a surfboard. Popping up can be practiced in the sand before entering the water.

Fact

When you stand on the board, your **stance** will be "goofy" or "regular." Goofy is when your right foot is in front. Regular is when your left foot is in front.

Fact

Remember the three Ps: persistence, practice, and patience!

Learning to ride on smaller, rolling waves is best. You will paddle out past where the waves break and wait for a good wave.

As a good wave approaches you, paddle hard toward shore. When you feel the wave lift your board, pop up to your feet, balance, and try to ride the wave.

Fact

Most people can learn the basics of longboarding within about one week of consistent practice. However, it takes a long time to master your skills!

FOR YOUR SAFETY

Longboarding is fun, but it can be dangerous if you are not prepared.

Safety Chart

- Always stretch before surfing
- Drink plenty of water
- Wear sunscreen
- Use the buddy system
- Wear your leash
- Respect other surfers
- Wear a wetsuit if needed

It is rare, but make sure to leave the water immediately if you see a shark.

Always wear a leash! A longboard is big, heavy, and can be very dangerous to yourself or others.

Fact

Getting hit by a surfboard is the most common type of surfing injury.

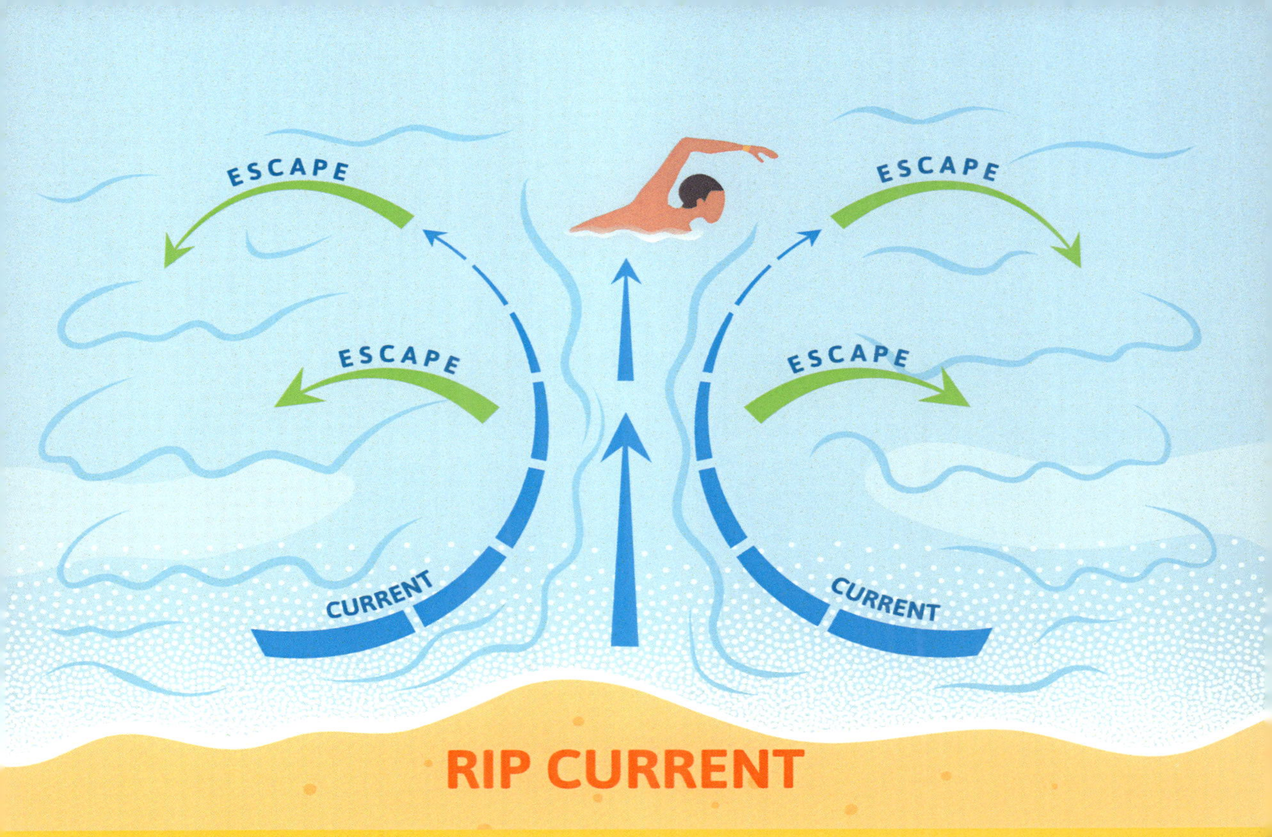

Before you enter the water, check the weather and the surf report. A surf report gives information about how safe the waves are. Surfers should also make sure they know what to do if they get stuck in a **rip current**.

Fact

Surfline is a popular website to check daily surf reports.

FAMOUS LONGBOARD SURFERS

There are many experienced and well-known longboarders around the world. Some of the best include Lance Carson, Nat Young, Josie Prendergast, and Kelia Moniz.

Kelia Moniz

Fact

The World Surf League (WSL) is an organization for professional and competitive surfing. It holds four international longboard surfing events each year to determine the world champions.

Taylor Jensen

In 2024, the WSL Men's Longboard World Champion was Taylor Jensen. The women's champion was Rachael Tilly. Both surfers are from the U.S.

RESPECTING OUR OCEANS

Our oceans make up 70 percent of Earth's surface. They are very important to all living creatures all over the world. They even generate half of the oxygen we breathe.

Fact

Millions of people depend on the ocean as their main food source.

Pollution is one of the main threats to the world's oceans. Surfers can show respect by always picking up their trash and joining local beach cleanups.

Fact

Taking care of the oceans is important. You can join an organization, such as the Surfrider Foundation, that is dedicated to the protection and enjoyment of the world's oceans.

Our oceans are beautiful, but they can also be very dangerous. The power of waves should be understood and respected by all surfers.

For many surfers, longboarding is a way of life. Everyone is welcome to give it a try. Paddle out and hang ten—the waves are waiting!

Glossary

ancient (eyn-shuhnt): Very old; existing a long time ago

balance (bal-uhns): Your ability to remain steady and upright

buoyancy (boi-uhn-see): The ability to stay afloat

leash (leesh): A strap or cord that is attached to a part of the body and the surfboard while surfing

pollution (puh-loo-shuhn): Harmful materials that damage or contaminate the air, water, and soil

rash guard (rash-gahrd): A fitted shirt worn while surfing to protect the skin from the Sun and from rough surfaces

reefs (reefs): Strips of rock, sand, or coral close to the surface of the ocean

rip current (rip-kur-uhnt): A strong flow of water running from a beach back to the open ocean

stance (stans): The way someone stands

surfing (surf-ing): To balance on a surfboard and ride the crest of a breaking wave toward shore

wetsuit (wet-soot): A close-fitting suit, usually made of a type of rubber called neoprene, that is worn in cold water to retain body heat